Could a Mouse Push a Car?

by Ms. Lewis' class
with Tony Stead

capstone

What Is a Force?

by Kaita

A force is a push or a pull. When a basketball player is trying to shoot the ball, he or she pushes the ball through the air. The push is the force.

You can also use force to push a cart while shopping. You can push the cart forward or pull it backward.

We wondered if a little mouse could ever use force to push a big car. We decided to find out more about forces to answer the question.

Push
Pull

The First Law of Motion

by Grace and Audrick

Isaac Newton was a scientist. He wanted to find out why things move the way they do. He came up with three laws of motion. Newton's First Law of Motion says:

- An object will stay in the same place unless another force acts on it.
- A moving object will keep moving unless another force makes it stop or change direction.

Every object in the universe has forces acting on it.

A ball at rest will keep resting unless something pushes or pulls on it. If you kick a ball, it will keep flying through the air until another force acts on it. The other force could be gravity or friction.

How Do Forces Affect Motion?

by Brooke

Forces make things move or make things stop moving. Forces can make things change direction or change speed, too.

For example, let's say someone is throwing a ball. The ball will move unless something is blocking its movement. If you throw hard, that is a big force, and the ball will go a long way. If you throw with a small force, the ball will only go a short way.

Another example is someone rolling a skateboard down a hill and it bumps into a rock in its path. The rock will push against the skateboard, and then the skateboard will change direction, stop, or slow down. So the force of the rock changes the movement of the skateboard!

skateboard
rock

How Does Friction Affect Motion?

by Jonny and Malia

Friction is created when two objects rub together. Friction is a force that slows things down until they stop.

One example of how friction affects motion is when you are sliding down a hill on cardboard. The gravitational pull on the Earth is what causes you to move.

There is friction between the cardboard and the grass. You slow down and then stop. If there was no friction, you would keep sliding until you made friction by putting your feet on the ground.

Another example is when you are riding a bike down a very steep hill way too fast, and you use the brakes. When you put on the brakes, you are causing friction between the brakes and the wheels. The friction makes you slow down and stop.

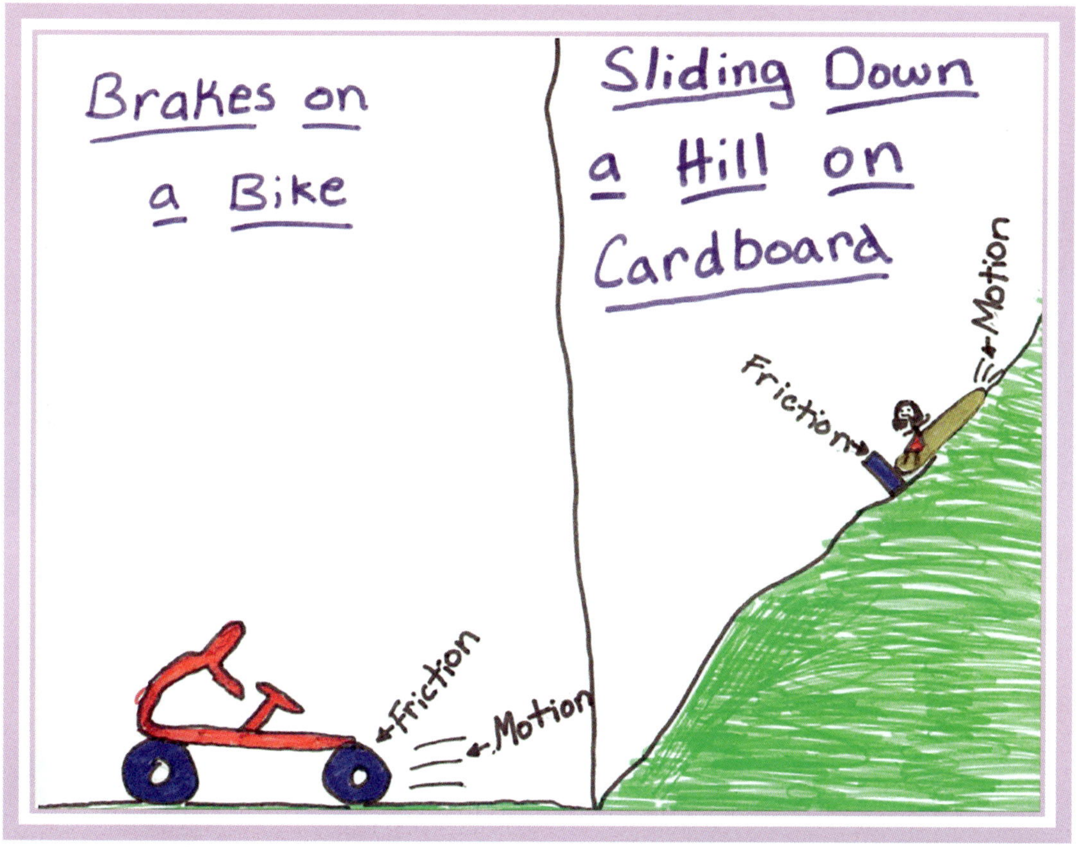

What Is Gravity?

by Henry and Serena

Gravity is the force that pulls us to the ground. Without gravity, we would float right away. Objects would float, too. We would float out of the window!

On Earth we are lucky to have gravity. Could you imagine our world without gravity? We would all float! Your clothes would float, your bed, everything!

Did You Know?

On bigger planets, the pull of gravity is stronger. If you weigh 60 pounds on Earth, you would weigh 152 pounds on Jupiter. This is because the pull of gravity on Jupiter is stronger.

illustrated by George

How Do Magnets Create Force?

by Ava and Gracie

A magnet is a rock or piece of metal that can pull certain kinds of metal toward it.

Magnets have two poles, a north pole and a south pole. The poles create a magnetic force. A magnetic force is the power to push or pull iron or steel together or apart. If you bring a north pole and a south pole together, the magnetic force pulls them together. If you bring the same poles together, the force repels the magnets. This means they push each other apart.

Magnetic forces can hold pictures on a refrigerator, and they help keep your refrigerator door closed or make it hard to open. People even use magnets on roller coasters to make you go really fast or to stop the roller coaster.

What Simple Machines Use Force?

by Joshua

Simple machines are gadgets that make jobs easier. Lots of things you don't expect are simple machines.

A ramp is a simple machine. You can push something up a ramp. The push is a force.

Door handles allow you to open doors. You push the handle, which is the force! Door handles also have screws. The screws hold the handle to the door! Screws are simple machines, too.

You pedal a bicycle. You push the pedals with your legs. This moves the wheels using a chain. Pushing the pedals is a force.

Wheels and ramps make it easier to move things. They turn small forces into bigger forces.

Can a Mouse Push a Car?

A mouse is really little. It is not strong and cannot make enough force by itself to move a car. Let's think how it could be possible.

The good thing is that the car has wheels. Wheels are simple machines and they make things easier to push. If a mouse got lots and lots of other mice to help, they could make enough force to push the car. If the mouse got a very strong magnet, it could pull a car toward it. That could beat gravity and friction.

So maybe, with some help, a mouse could push a car. But it would be a tough job!

illustrated by George